Cyber
Jokes

The Funniest Stuff on the Internet

by Doug Mayer

Andrews and McMeel
A Universal Press Syndicate Company
Kansas City

 For information, write Andrews and McMeel, a Universal Press Syndicate Company, 4520 Main Street, Kansas City, Missouri 64111.

Library of Congress Cataloging-in-Publication Data:

Cyber Jokes : the funniest stuff on the Internet / [compiled] by Doug Mayer.

p. cm.
ISBN 0-8362-1075-1
1. Wit and humor. 2. Internet (computer network)—Humor.
I. Mayer, Doug.
PN6231.I62C93 1996
818'.540208—dc20 96-401
CIP

All of the text in this book has been obtained from publically accessible on-line sources, and has been included to demonstrate the variety of work that is available on the Internet.

ATTENTION: SCHOOLS AND BUSINESSES

Andrews and McMeel books are available at quantity discounts with bulk purchase for educational, business, or sales promotional use. For information, please write to: Special Sales Department, Andrews and McMeel, 4520 Main Street, Kansas City, Missouri 64111.

Introduction

We've all heard the hype: The Internet will revolutionize the way we interact—both in business and how we stay in touch with friends, relatives, and schoolmates. Information will bounce around at the speed of light, making each of us countless times more productive. Or so they say.

Thankfully, there are thousands of anonymous heroes out there—net users who are saving us from this hyperproductive destiny, and making the Internet plenty of fun in the process. They are the creators of the "Microsoft Bids to Acquire Catholic Church" press release and important treatises like "Important Breaking Sesame Street News" *(page 93)* *and* "How to Remove a Dead Whale" *(page 18)*.

The Internet is vast, and we have only tapped the surface of the insanity that lurks around its edges. E-mail us your contributions for future issues at ***cyberjokes@aol.com.*** In the meantime, watch out for falling whale blubber, crack-addicted puppets, and please, don't try all thirty-four fun things to do in an elevator.

It is with great trepidation that I thank the following contributors: Dave Medvitz, Jon Martinson, Scott Balderson, Craig Healy, Ed Hutchinson, Greg Galer, Laurie

Sale, Joe Dillon, and Margaret Wold-Sackey. This crew of cyberhumorists successfully scoured the Internet for its funny, bizarre and twisted offerings—all when they were ostensibly hard at work as a teacher, researcher, financial manager, engineer, public relations specialist, or computer programmer. So much for that vaunted productivity—let's hope your bosses never see this book!

—Doug Mayer

Microsoft Bids to Acquire Catholic Church

VATICAN CITY (AP)—**In a joint press conference** in St. Peter's Square this morning, Microsoft Corporation and the Vatican announced that the Redmond, Washington, software giant will acquire the Roman Catholic Church in exchange for an unspecified number of shares of Microsoft common stock. If the deal goes through, it will be the first time a computer software company has acquired a major world religion.

With the acquisition, Pope John Paul II will become the senior vice president of the combined company's new Religious Software Division, while Microsoft senior vice presidents Michael Maples and Steven Ballmer will be invested in the College of Cardinals, said Microsoft chairman Bill Gates.

"We expect a lot of growth in the religious market in the next five to ten years," said Gates. "The combined resources of Microsoft and the Catholic Church will allow us to make religion easier and more fun for a broader range of people."

Through the Microsoft Network, the company's new on-line service, "we will make the sacraments available on-line for the first time" and revive the popular pre-counter-Reformation practice of selling indulgences, said Gates. "You can get Communion, confess your sins, receive absolution—even reduce your time in purgatory—all without leaving your home." A new software application, Microsoft Church, will include a macro language that you can program to download heavenly graces automatically while you are away from your computer.

An estimated seventeen thousand people attended the announcement in St. Peter's Square, watching on a sixty-foot screen as comedian Don Novello—in character as Father Guido Sarducci—hosted the event, which was broadcast by satellite to seven hundred sites worldwide.

Pope John Paul II said little during the announcement. When Novello chided Gates, "Now I guess you get to wear one of these pointy hats," the crowd roared, but the pontiff's smile seemed strained.

The deal grants Microsoft exclusive electronic rights to the Bible and the Vatican's prized art collection, which includes works by such masters as Michelangelo and da Vinci. But critics say Microsoft will face stiff challenges if it attempts to limit competitors' access to these key intellectual properties.

"The Jewish people invented the look and feel of the holy scriptures," said Rabbi David Gottschalk of Philadelphia. "You take the parting of the Red Sea—we had that thousands of years before the Catholics came on the scene."

But others argue that the Catholic and Jewish faiths both draw on a common Abrahamic heritage. "The Catholic Church has just been more successful in marketing it to a larger audience," notes Notre Dame theologian Father Kenneth Madigan. Over the last two thousand years, the Catholic Church's market share has increased dramatically, while Judaism, which was the first to offer many of the concepts now touted by Christianity, lags behind.

Historically, the church has a reputation as an aggressive competitor, leading crusades to pressure people to upgrade to Catholicism, and entering into exclusive licensing arrangements in various kingdoms whereby all subjects were instilled with Catholicism, whether or not they planned to use it. Today Christianity is available from several denominations, but the Catholic version is still the most widely used. The church's mission is to reach "the four corners of the earth," echoing Microsoft's vision of "a computer on every desktop and in every home."

Gates described Microsoft's long-term strategy to develop a scalable religious architecture that will support all religions through emulation. A single core religion will be offered with a choice of interfaces according to the religion desired—"One religion, a couple of different implementations," said Gates.

The Microsoft move could spark a wave of mergers and acquisitions, according to Herb Peters, a spokesman for the U.S. Southern Baptist Conference, as other churches scramble to strengthen their position in the increasingly competitive religious market.

By Hank Vorjes

Why God Never Received Tenure at the University

1. Because He had only one major publication.
2. And it was in Hebrew.
3. And it had no references.
4. And it was not published in a refereed journal.
5. And some even doubt He wrote it himself.
6. It may be true that He created the world, but what has He published/done since then?
7. His cooperative efforts have been quite limited.
8. The scientific community has had a hard time replicating His results.
9. He never applied to the Ethics Board for permission to use human subjects.
10. When one experiment went awry, He tried to cover it up by drowning the subjects.
11. When subjects did not behave as predicted, He deleted them from the sample.
12. He rarely came to class; just told His students to read the Book.
13. Some say He had His son teach the class.
14. He expelled His first two students for learning.
15. Though there were only ten requirements, most students failed His tests.
16. His office hours were infrequent and usually held on a mountaintop.

Is There a Santa Claus?

1. **No known species of reindeer can fly.** But there are three hundred thousand species of living organisms yet to be classified, and while most of these are insects and germs, this does not completely rule out flying reindeer, which only Santa has ever seen.

2. **There are two billion children** (persons under eighteen) in the world. But since Santa doesn't (appear) to handle the Muslim, Hindu, Jewish, and Buddhist children, that reduces the workload to 15 percent of the total—378 million, according to the Population Reference Bureau. At an average (census) rate of 3.5 children per household, that's 91.8 million homes. One presumes there's at least one good child in each.

3. **Santa has thirty-one hours** of Christmas to work with, thanks to the different time zones and the rotation of the earth, assuming he travels east to west (which seems logical). This works out to 822.6 visits per second. This is to say that for each Christian household with good children, Santa has 1/1,000th of a second to park, hop out of the sleigh, jump down the chimney, fill the stockings, distribute the remaining presents under the tree, eat whatever snacks

have been left, get back up the chimney, get back into the sleigh, and move on to the next house. Assuming that these 91.8 million stops are evenly distributed around the earth (which, of course, we know to be false, but for the purposes of our calculations we will accept), we are now talking about .78 miles per household, a total trip of 75.5 million miles, not counting stops to do what most of us must do at least once every thirty-one hours, plus feeding, etc. This means that Santa's sleigh is moving at 650 miles per second, three thousand times the speed of sound. For purposes of comparison, the fastest man-made vehicle on earth, the Ulysses space probe, moves at a poky 27.4 miles per second—a conventional reindeer can run, tops, fifteen miles per hour.

4. **The payload on the sleigh** adds another interesting element. Assuming that each child gets nothing more than a medium-size Lego set (two pounds), the sleigh is carrying 321,300 tons, not counting Santa, who is invariably described as overweight. On land, conventional reindeer can pull no more than three hundred pounds. Even granting that "flying reindeer" (see point no. 1) could pull ten times the normal amount, we cannot do the job with eight, or even nine. We need 214,200 reindeer. This increases the payload—not even counting

the weight of the sleigh—to 353,430 tons. Again, for comparison—this is four times the weight of the *Queen Elizabeth.*

5. Three hundred fifty-three thousand tons traveling at 650 miles per second creates enormous air resistance—this will heat the reindeer up in the same fashion as spacecraft reentering Earth's atmosphere. The lead pair of reindeer will absorb 14.3 quintillion joules of energy. Per second. Each. In short, they will burst into flame almost instantaneously, exposing the reindeer behind them, and create deafening sonic booms in their wake. The entire reindeer team will be vaporized within 4.26-thousandths of a second. Santa, meanwhile, will be subjected to centrifugal forces 17,500.06 times greater than gravity. A 250-pound Santa (which seems ludicrously slim) would be pinned to the back of his sleigh by 4,315,015 pounds of force.

In conclusion—if Santa ever did deliver presents on Christmas Eve, he's dead now.

And the Less Factual Rebuttal . . .

Come on, ya gotta believe! I mean, if you can handle flying furry animals, then it's only a small step to the rest. For example:

1. ***As admitted,*** it is possible that a flying reindeer can be found. I would agree that it would be quite an unusual find, but they might exist.

2. ***You've relied on cascading assumptions.*** For example, you have assumed a uniform distribution of children across homes. Toronto/Yorkville, or Toronto/Cabbagetown, or other yuppie neighborhoods, have probably less than the average (and don't forget the DINK and SINK homes—Double Income No Kids, Single Income No Kids), while the families with 748 starving children that they keep showing on Vision TV while trying to pick my pocket would skew that 15 percent of homes down a few percent.

3. ***You've also assumed*** that each home that has kids would have at least one good kid. What if antiselection applies, and homes with good kids tend to have more than their share of good kids, and other homes have nothing except terrorists in diapers? Let's drop that number of homes down a few more percent.

4. ***Santa would have to Fed-Ex*** a number of packages ahead of time, since he would not be able to fly into air force bases, or into tower-controlled areas near airports. He'd get shot at over certain sections of the Middle East, and the no-fly zones in Iraq, so he'd probably use DHL there. Subtract some more homes.

5. ***I just barely passed physics*** and only read Stephen Hawking's book once, but I recall that there is some Einsteinian theory that says time does strange things as you move faster. In fact, when you go faster than the speed of light time runs backward, if you do a straight-line projection, connect the dots, and just ignore any singularity you might find right at the speed of light. And don't say you can't go faster than the speed of light because I've seen it done on TV. Jean-Luc doesn't have reindeer but he does have matter-antimatter warp engines and a holodeck and that's good enough for me. So Santa could go faster than light, visit all the good children not uniformly distributed by either concentration in each home or by number of children per household, and get home before he left so he can digest all those stale cookies and warm milk. *Yech.*

6. ***Aha, you say,*** Jean-Luc has matter-antimatter warp engines, Santa only has reindeer, so where does he get the power to move that fast? You calculated the answer! The lead pair of reindeer will absorb 14.3 quintillion joules of energy. Per second. Each. This is an ample supply of energy for the maneuvering, acceleration, etc., that would be required of the loaded sleigh. The reindeer don't evaporate or incinerate because of this energy, they accelerate. What do you think they have

antlers for, fighting over females? Think of antlers as furry solar array panels.

7. ***If that's not enough,*** watch the news on the twenty-fourth at eleven o'clock. NORADM (which may be one of the few government agencies with more than three initials in its name, and therefore it must be more trustworthy than the rest) tracks Santa every year, and I've seen the radar shots of him approaching my house from the direction of the North Pole. They haven't bomarck'd him yet, so they must believe too, right?

Ten Most Unsuccessful Pickup Lines

1. Would you like to see my boa constrictor?
2. Is that a false nose?
3. You look like a hooker I knew in Fresno.
4. I'm drunk.
5. Hi, my friends call me Creepy.
6. Would you like to come to a party in my toolshed?
7. I just threw up.
8. You're ugly, but you intrigue me.
9. I had to find out what kind of woman would go out dressed like that.
10. I know my future ex-girlfriend is in here somewhere!

How to Remove a Dead Whale

I am absolutely not making this incident up; in fact, I have it all on videotape. The tape is from a local TV news show in Oregon, which sent a reporter out to cover the removal of a forty-five-foot, eight-ton, dead whale that washed up on the beach. The responsibility for getting rid of the carcass was placed on the Oregon State Highway Division, apparently on the theory that highways and whales are very similar in the sense of being large objects.

So anyway, the highway engineers hit upon the plan—remember, I am not making this up—of blowing up the whale with dynamite. The thinking is that the whale would be blown into small pieces, which would be eaten by seagulls, and that would be that. A textbook whale removal.

So they moved the spectators back up the beach, put a half-ton of dynamite next to the whale and set it off. I am probably not guilty of understatement when I say that what follows, on the videotape, is the most wonderful event in the history of the universe. First you see the whale carcass disappear in a huge blast of smoke and flame. Then you hear the happy spectators shouting "Yay!" and "Whee!" Then, suddenly, the crowd's tone changes. You hear a new sound like "splud." You hear a woman's voice shouting, "Here come pieces of . . . My God!" Something smears the camera lens.

Later, the reporter explains: "The humor of the entire situation suddenly gave way to a run for survival as huge chunks of whale blubber fell everywhere." One piece caved in the roof of a car parked more than a quarter of a mile away. Remaining on the beach were several rotting whale sectors the size of condominium units. There was no sign of the seagulls who had no doubt permanently relocated to Brazil.

This is a very sobering videotape. Here at the institute we watch it often, especially at picnics. But this is no time for gaiety. This is a time to get hold of the folks at the Oregon State Highway Division and ask them, when they get done cleaning up the beaches, to give us an estimate on the U.S. Capitol.

—Tom Mahoney,
Coast Guard Sqn.I/Div.13 CatLo

The Definitive List of Bumper Sticker Philosophy

BUREAUCRACY: A METHOD FOR TRANSFORMING ENERGY INTO SOLID WASTE

LEMMINGS DON'T GROW OLDER, THEY JUST DIE

BE REALISTIC: PLAN FOR A MIRACLE

LOVE THY NEIGHBOR, TUNE THY PIANO

REAL PEOPLE WEAR FAKE FURS

YOU HAVE A SEATBELT; HAS IT HUGGED YOU TODAY?

SPEED PAYS—THE DOCTOR, THE HOSPITAL, THE MORTUARY

ILLITERATE? WRITE FOR FREE HELP

MY OTHER CAR IS A REAL OTA

EARTH FIRST! WE'LL LOG THE OTHER PLANETS LATER

ONE SOVIET INVASION CAN RUIN YOUR WHOLE DAY

BEWARE OF QUANTUM DUCKS, QUARK! QUARK!

SUPPORT MENTAL HEALTH, OR I'LL KILL YOU!

HELP STAMP OUT INTOLERANCE!

I'M NOT FOR APATHY, AND I'M NOT AGAINST IT.

HAVE YOU HUGGED YOUR MONEY TODAY?

PROSPERITY IS OUR GOD-GIVEN RIGHT

SAVE THE CHOCOLATE MOOSE!

ARCHAEOLOGISTS WILL DATE ANY OLD THING

I REFUSE TO PARTICIPATE IN THE RECESSION

I BRAKE FOR BRICK WALLS

FIGHT ORGANIZED CRIME, STAMP OUT THE IRS

I CANNOT BE FIRED. SLAVES HAVE TO BE SOLD

ESCHEW OBFUSCATION

THE HIGHWAY OF LIFE IS ALWAYS UNDER CONSTRUCTION

DOES THE NAME PAVLOV RING A BELL?

WELCOME TO LOS ANGELES—NOW GO HOME

DO LOS ANGELES A FAVOR: WHEN YOU LEAVE, TAKE SOMEONE WITH YOU

I'M SO POOR, I CAN'T EVEN PAY ATTENTION!

I LOVE, I OWE, SO OFF TO WORK I GO

WARP 6. A LAW WE CAN LIVE WITH

THE SAN DIEGO FREEWAY . . . OFFICIAL PARKING LOT OF THE 1984 OLYMPICS!

HAVE YOU HARASSED A TOURIST TODAY?

THE TROUBLE WITH POLITICAL JOKES IS THEY GET ELECTED

PASS WITH CARE, DRIVER CHEWING TOBACCO

WHEN I GROW UP, I WANT TO BE A PORSCHE

HONK IF YOU'RE CUTE, RICH, AND LOVE HORSES

LEAVE ME ALONE, I'M HAVING A CRISIS

THE BEST THING TO SPEND ON YOUR CHILDREN IS TIME

I HATE BUMPER STICKERS

THREE GOOD THINGS ABOUT SCHOOL: JUNE, JULY, AUGUST

SUPPORT YOUR RIGHT TO ARM BEARS!

IGNORE APATHY

I. Thou shalt not worship or idolize the Purple Demon known to thee as B'harnee no matter how heavily he is merchandised, lest thy brain become spongified.

The Ten Commandments (Slightly Revised for the '90s)

II. Thou mayest use the name of B'harnee in vain, if necessary, but do not repeat the name often, for it gives the beast power and makes intelligent people wish to puke.

III. Thou shalt honor the Jihad and all who support it, for it is through their efforts that the world shall be saved from the Purple Menace.

IV. Thou shalt observe and obey the canon known as the Threefold Truth, and keep it holy.

V. Thou shalt feel free to viciously kill B'harnee in any way thou findest convenient and effective, as well as any unrepentant followers of the Purple Demon.

VI. Thou shalt not engage in any sexual relation with beings who are not human, are brightly colored, and whose minds are as simple and pliable as Silly Putty.

VII. Thou shalt not covet or purchase B'harnee merchandise, no matter how much thy children may whine and scream.

VIII. Thou shalt not steal, or allow anyone else to steal or control another's mind using the seductive powers of the Purple Menace.

IX. Thou shalt do everything in thy power to stop the lies spread by Sponge-Minions concerning the Evil One, Teach the Threefold Truth to everyone thy can, and thou shalt emerge triumphant.

X. Never forget: B'harnee must be destroyed. All else is immaterial.

Top Ten Things People Think the "95" in Windows 95 Really Stands for:

1. *The number of floppies it will ship on.*
2. *The percentage of people who will have to upgrade their hardware.*
3. *The number of megabytes of disk space required.*
4. *The number of pages in the Easy-Install version of the manual.*
5. *The percentage of existing programs that won't run under the new operating system.*
6. *The number of minutes to install.*
7. *The number of calls for technical support before it will work.*
8. *The total number of people who actually pay for the upgrade.*
9. *The required speed of the CPU in MHz.*
10. *The year it was due to ship.*

New Barbie!

(LOS ANGELES)—**Mattel announces** their new line of Barbie products, the "Hacker Barbie." These new dolls will be released next month. The aim of these dolls is to reverse the stereotype that women are numerophobic, computer-illiterate, and academically challenged.

This new line of Barbie dolls comes equipped with Barbie's very own xterminal and UNIX documentation as well as ORA's "In a Nutshell" series. The Barbie is robed in a dirty button-up shirt and a pair of worn-out jeans with Casio all-purpose watches and thick glasses that can set ants on fire. Pocket protectors and HP calculators optional. The new Barbie has the incredible ability to stare at the screen without blinking her eyes and to go without eating or drinking for twelve hours straight. Her vocabulary mainly consists of technical terms such as "IP address," "TCP/IP," "kernel," "NP-complete," and "Alpha AXPs."

"We are very excited about this product," said John Olson, marketing executive, "and we hope that the Hacker Barbie will offset the damage incurred by the mathophobic Barbie." A year ago, Mattel released Barbie dolls that said, "Math is hard," with a condescending companion Ken. The Hacker Barbie's Ken is an incompetent consultant who frequently asks Barbie for help.

The leading feminists are equally excited about this new line of Barbie dolls. Naomi Wuuf says, "I believe that these new dolls will finally terminate the notion that women are inherently inferior when it comes to mathematics and the sciences. However, I feel that Ken's hierarchical superiority would simply reinforce the patriarchy and oppress the masses." Mattel made no comment.

Parents, however, are worried that they would become technologically behind by comparison to the children when the Hacker Barbie comes out. "My daughter Jenny plays with the prototype Hacker Barbie over yonder for two days," says Mrs. Mary Carlson of Oxford, Mississippi, "and as y'all know, she now pays my credit card bill. Ain't got no idea how she duz it, but she surely duz it. I jus don't wanna be looked upon as a dumb mama." Mattel will be offering free training courses for those who purchase the Hacker Barbie.

The future Hacker Barbie will include several variations to deal with the complex aspects of Barbie. "Hacker Barbie Goes to Jail" will teach computer ethics to youngsters, while "Barbie Rites Like Biff!!!" will serve as an introduction to expository writing.

Fun Things to Do in an Elevator

1. *Whistle the first seven notes of "It's a Small World" incessantly.*
2. *Crack open your briefcase or purse, and while peering inside ask, "Got enough air in there?"*
3. *Offer name tags to everyone getting on the elevator. Wear yours upside-down.*
4. *Stand silent and motionless in the corner, facing the wall, without getting off.*
5. *When arriving at your floor, grunt and strain to yank the doors open, then act embarrassed when they open themselves.*
6. *Lean over to another passenger and whisper, "Noogie patrol coming!"*
7. *Greet everyone getting on the elevator with a warm handshake and ask them to call you Admiral.*
8. *On the highest floor, hold the doors open and demand that it stay open until you hear the penny you dropped down the shaft go "plink" at the bottom.*
9. *Blow your nose and offer to show the contents of your Kleenex to the other passengers.*
10. *Stare grinning at another passenger for a while, and then announce: "I've got new socks on!"*

11. Meow occasionally.

12. Bet the other passengers you can fit a quarter in your nose. Curse anyone who doesn't express an interest in your talent. Complain about the downfall of society's interest in the performing arts.

13. Show the other passengers a wound, and ask if it looks infected. Ask if they will help you use the emergency phone to get medical attention. If they refuse, ask them to at least kiss your cut "like Mom used to."

14. Sing "Mary Had a Little Lamb" while continually pushing buttons.

15. Carry a cooler that says "human head" on the side.

16. Stare at another passenger for a while, then announce, "You're one of them!" and move to the far corner of the elevator.

17. Ask each passenger getting on if you can push the button for them.

18. Ask each passenger getting off if you can push the button for them.

19. When the elevator is silent, look around and ask, "Is that your beeper?" Demand a strip search of all passengers when no one confesses to having a beeper.

20. Play the harmonica. Ask your fellow passengers if they happen to have a can of beans and some firewood.

21. Say "Ding!" at each floor.

22. Lean against the button panel.

23. Say "I wonder what all these do?" and push the red buttons.

24. Listen to the elevator walls with a stethoscope, shaking your head sadly.

25. Draw a little square on the floor with chalk and announce to the other passengers that this is your "personal space."

26. Bring a chair along.

27. Carry a blanket and clutch it protectively. Refuse to discuss it.

28. Make explosion noises when anyone presses a button.

29. Wear "X-Ray Specs" and leer suggestively at the other passengers.

30. Stare at your thumb and say, "I think it's getting larger."

31. Count down "5 . . . 4 . . . 3 . . . 2 . . . 1 . . ." and then suddenly duck.

32. Sell motion-sickness medicine.

33. Eat butter.

34. Walk in, look confused, and ask, "Where's the pedals?"

Microsoft "Windows 95" Stuns World

WASHINGTON (AP)—**Fans and detractors** of the long-awaited Microsoft Windows 95 have been stunned and amazed by the incredible events surrounding the August 24 release. Windows 95 has been hailed by industry giant Pierson Holcombe Pewter as "the most advanced operating system ever produced." But even he could not have predicted yesterday's events.

It began when peace was declared in Bosnia. Said Ahmad G'Hui, spokesperson for the Serbs, "Now that [Windows 95] has been released, we just don't see any reason to fight each other. This is an amazing product."

Then France announced its intention to stop all testing of nuclear weapons. "We used to think that our national boundaries were of utmost import. To safeguard them, it was necessary to continue testing [nuclear weapons]," said Jacques Fenetre of the French government. "The Microsoft Network™ has changed all of that. It's such a small planet!"

On the other side of the "small planet," George Bush and Saddam Hussein met face-to-face for the first time. After a tense greeting, they started sharing notes about their experiences as Windows 95 beta-testers. Soon the two lifelong enemies were laughing and chatting like old friends. In a startling display of candor, Hussein said, "If I hadn't been so frustrated with the beta,

I'd have backed off from Kuwait much sooner." Bush laughed and commiserated with Hussein, saying, "Well, Saddam, let's play some FreeCell!"

Oil prices dropped as OPEC transferred their accounting software to the new platform. Loggers in the United States' Pacific Northwest turned their axes in for spades after seeing a Microsoft video of spotted owls using Windows 95. In an economic shocker, the peso reversed its downward spiral due to huge Windows 95 sales in Acapulco and Mexico City. On the health front, Hildegard Wicca, a housewife in Boston, Massachusetts, reports that Windows 95 has removed her facial warts. "I sat down in front of the computer, pressed 'Start,' and felt something odd on my face. When I looked in a mirror, my warts were gone!"

Even more amazing is the story of Mark Cense, the Los Alamos man who was reported last week as having an incurable, fatal form of cancer. His doctors were amazed yesterday when, after simply buying Windows 95 at the local Computer Universe store, his cancer went into remission.

When asked for a comment on these almost miraculous events, Microsoft's Bill Gates, recently declared to be the richest man in the United States, replied, "If you think this is good, just wait until you see Windows 97!"

Reports that China's release of dissident Harry Wu was contingent on his returning with "as many copies of Windows 95 as he can carry" are unconfirmed at this time.

Ten Signs You've Watched Too Much Star Trek

1. You send weekly love letters to the actress who played the green-skinned Orion slave girl in episode no. 7.
2. You pull the legs off of your hamster so you'll have a Trible.
3. You try to join the navy just so you could serve aboard the *Enterprise.*
4. Your wife left you because you wanted her to dress like a Klingon and torture you for information.
5. You went to San Francisco to see if you might bump into Kirk and crew while they were in the twentieth century looking for a whale.
6. Your college thesis was a comparison of the illustrious careers of T. J. Hooker and James T. Kirk.
7. You fly into a homicidal rage anytime people say, "*Star Trek*? Isn't that the one with Luke Skywalker?"
8. You have no life.
9. You recognize more than four references on this list.
10. You join NASA, hijack a shuttle, and head for the coordinates you calculated for the planet Vulcan.

You Say Suicide, I Say Homicide . . .

At the 1994 annual awards dinner given by the American Association for Forensic Science, AAFS president Don Harper Mills astounded his audience in San Diego with the legal complications of a bizarre death. Here is the story:

On 23 March 1994, the medical examiner viewed the body of Ronald Opus and concluded that he died from a shotgun wound to the head. The decedent had jumped from the top of a ten-story building intending to commit suicide (he left a note indicating his despondency). As he fell past the ninth floor, his life was interrupted by a shotgun blast through a window, which killed him instantly. Neither the shooter nor the decedent was aware that a safety net had been erected at the eighth-floor level to protect some window washers and that Opus would not have been able to complete his suicide anyway because of this.

Ordinarily, Dr. Mills continued, a person who sets out to commit suicide ultimately succeeds, even though the mechanism might not be what he intended. That Opus was shot on the way to certain death nine stories below probably would not have changed his mode of death from suicide to homicide. But the fact that his suicidal intent would not have been successful caused the medical examiner to feel that he had a homicide on his hands.

The room on the ninth floor whence the shotgun blast emanated was occupied by an elderly man and his wife. They were arguing and he was threatening her with the shotgun. He was so upset that, when he pulled the trigger, he completely missed his wife and pellets went through the window striking Opus. When one intends to kill subject A but kills subject B in the attempt, one is guilty of the murder of subject B. When confronted with this charge, the old man and his wife were both adamant that neither knew that the shotgun was loaded. The old man said it was his long-standing habit to threaten his wife with the unloaded shotgun. He had no intention to murder her—therefore, the killing of Opus appeared to be an accident. That is, the gun had been accidentally loaded.

The continuing investigation turned up a witness who saw the old couple's son loading the shotgun approximately six weeks prior to the fatal incident. It transpired that the old lady had cut off her son's financial support and the son, knowing the propensity of his father to use the shotgun threateningly, loaded the gun with the expectation that his father would shoot his mother. The case now becomes one of murder on the part of the son for the death of Ronald Opus. There was an exquisite twist when further investigation revealed that the son, one Ronald Opus, had become increasingly despondent over the failure of his attempt to engineer his mother's murder. This led him to jump off the ten-story building on March 23, only to be killed by a shotgun blast through a ninth-story window. The medical examiner closed the case as a suicide.

Unclassifiable Classifieds

The following excerpts were culled from the classified sections of newspapers from across the country:

Wanted: Fifty girls for stripping machine operators in factory.

We do not tear your clothing with machinery. We do it carefully by hand.

Dog for sale: Eats anything and is fond of children.

For Sale—Eight puppies from a German Shepherd and an Alaskan Hussy.

Lost: Small apricot poodle. Reward. Neutered. Like one of the family.

Man wanted to work in dynamite factory. Must be willing to travel.

Used Cars: Why go elsewhere to be cheated? Come here first!

A superb and inexpensive restaurant. Fine food expertly served by waitresses in appetizing forms.

Dinner Special—Turkey $2.35; Chicken or Beef $2.25; Children $2.00.

For sale: An antique desk suitable for lady with thick legs and large drawers.

Four-poster bed, 101 years old. Perfect for antique lover.

Now is your chance to have your ears pierced and get an extra pair to take home, too.

For Sale. Three canaries of undermined sex.

Great Dames for sale.

Have several very old dresses from grandmother in beautiful condition.

Tired of cleaning yourself? Let me do it.

Vacation Special: Have your home exterminated.

If you think you've seen everything in Paris, visit the Père-Lachaise Cemetery. It boasts such immortals as Molière, Jean de la Fontaine, and Chopin.

Mt. Kilimanjaro, the breathtaking backdrop for the Serena Lodge. Swim in the lovely pool while you drink it all in. The hotel has bowling alleys, tennis courts, comfortable beds, and other athletic facilities.

Sheer stockings. Designed for fancy dress, but so serviceable that lots of women wear nothing else.

Stock up and save. Limit: one.

We build bodies that last a lifetime.

For Rent: Six-room hated apartment.

Wanted: chambermaid in rectory. Love in, $200 a month. References required.

Christmas tag sale. Handmade gifts for the hard-to-find person.

Modular Sofas. Only $299. For rest or for play.

Wanted: Hair-cutter. Excellent growth potential.

Wanted. Man to take care of cow that does not smoke or drink.

Three-year-old teacher needed for preschool. Experience preferred.

Our experienced Mom will take care of your child. Fenced yard, meals, and smacks included.

Auto Repair Service. Free pick-up and delivery. Try us once, you'll never go anywhere again.

Illiterate? Write today for free help.

Girl wanted to assist magician in cutting-off-head illusion. Blue Cross and salary.

Mixing bowl set designed to please a cook with round bottom for efficient beating.

Semiannual after-Christmas sale.

We will oil your sewing machine and adjust tension in your home for $1.00.

News Flash!

In a surprise move, Microsoft chairman Bill Gates announced yesterday that he has purchased the entire calendar year of 1995. 1995 will be replaced instead by "Year-M" to be followed by actual 1995.

"Windows 95 was not going to ship on schedule," Gates said. "But we couldn't change the name again . . . people were starting to get confused. So instead of spending a lot of time and money on a new marketing campaign we decided just to buy 1995. That way we get an extra year to debug Windows and get it shipped for what will be the new 1995."

Microsoft arranged this coup by leveraging its financial assets to bail out the federal government and pay off the national debt. The IRS is being disbanded for next year, but taxes will be collected as usual with one change: All checks must be made payable to "Bill Gates."

A side benefit of this purchase is that Gates now owns the judicial branch for the duration of "Year-M." Speculators stated that Gates would likely use this opportunity to dismiss the numerous lawsuits pending against Microsoft. Gates apparently feels this would be cheaper than actually hiring lawyers to represent his rickety cases.

In a related story, God has filed suit against Gates because of his purchase, claiming time to be the sole property of God. In a countersuit, Gates claims God is a monopoly and demands that he be broken up into "deity conglomerates."

"Gosh," said Gates. "They broke up AT&T . . . why can't we break up God?"

Inside sources at Microsoft said that Gates was looking for an early resolution to the suit by hiring God as a programmer. Evidently, God has the exact profile that Gates is looking for in a programmer: He doesn't mind rainy climates, doesn't need any money, isn't married, and can work for at least six days without sleeping.

"If we could just get some employees like that," Gates lamented, "we would be able to ship Windows 95 on time."

You Did What?

The terse prose required for an insurance-form accident report can be quite a challenge for some people. The following excerpts represent the best of the genre, and capture the infinite potential of the human mind.

Coming home, I drove into the wrong house and collided with a tree I don't have.

The other car collided with mine without giving warning of its intentions.

I thought my window was down, but found it was up when I put my hand through it.

I told the police that I was uninjured. But on removing my hat, I found that I had a fractured skull.

I collided with a stationary truck coming the other way.

A truck backed through my windshield into my wife's face.

A pedestrian hit me and went under my car.

The guy was all over the road. I had to swerve a number of times before I hit him.

I pulled away from the side of the road, glanced at my mother-in-law, and headed over the embankment.

The gentleman behind me struck me on the backside. He went to rest in the bush with just his rear end showing.

In my attempt to kill a fly, I drove into a telephone pole.

The accident occurred when I was attempting to bring my car out of a skid by steering it into the other vehicle.

I had been learning to drive without power steering. I turned the wheel to what I thought was enough and found myself in a different direction going the opposite way.

I was on my way to the doctor's with rear end trouble when my universal joint gave way, causing me to have an accident.

As I approached the intersection, a stop sign suddenly appeared in a place where no stop sign had ever appeared before. I was unable to stop in time to avoid the accident.

To avoid hitting the bumper of the car in front, I struck the pedestrian.

My car was legally parked as it backed into the other vehicle.

An invisible car appeared out of nowhere, struck my vehicle, and vanished.

When I saw I could not avoid a collision, I stepped on the gas and crashed into the other vehicle.

The indirect cause of the accident was a little guy in a small car with a big mouth.

I saw the slow-moving, sad-faced old gentleman as he bounced off the hood of my car.

I was thrown from my car as it left the road. I was later found in a ditch by some stray cows.

The telephone pole was approaching fast. I was attempting to swerve out of its path when it struck my front end.

I saw her look at me twice; she appeared to be making slow progress when we met on impact.

No one was to blame for the accident but it never would have happened if the other driver had been alert.

I was unable to stop in time and my car crashed into the other vehicle. The driver and passengers then left immediately for a vacation with injuries.

I had been shopping for plants all day and was on my way home. As I reached an intersection, a hedge sprang up, obscuring my vision. I didn't see the other car.

I had been driving my car for forty years when I fell asleep at the wheel and had an accident.

I was sure the old fellow would never make it to the other side of the roadway when I struck him.

The pedestrian had no idea which direction to go, so I ran over him.

The trees were passing me in an orderly row at fifty miles per hour when suddenly one of them stepped out into my path.

I ran over a man, he admitted it was his fault since he had been knocked down before.

I ran into a lamppost that was obscured by human beings.

The accident was caused by me waving to the man I hit last week.

Cut down a tree in my backyard. Tree was supposed to go west, it went east.

We entered the house about midnight after going out for the evening; since I smelled something in the air, my fiancée wouldn't let me turn on the lights since if it was gas, the spark may ignite the gas, so I lit a match instead . . .

Ten Best Bumper Stickers on the Starship Enterprise

1. OUR OTHER STARSHIP SEPARATES INTO THREE PIECES!

2. ONE PHOTON TORPEDO CAN RUIN YOUR WHOLE DAY . . . THINK ABOUT IT.

3. HONK IF YOU'VE SLEPT WITH COMMANDER RIKER!

4. GUNS DON'T KILL PEOPLE . . . CLASS TWO PHASERS DO!

5. ZERO TO WARP 9.7 IN 13 SECONDS!

6. CAUTION . . . WE HAVE A TRIGGER HAPPY KLINGON AT TACTICAL.

7. IF YOU CAN READ THIS . . . DON'T YOU THINK YOU'RE A WEE BIT TOO CLOSE?

8. BLONDE BORGS HAVE THE SAME FUN.

9. WE BRAKE FOR CUBES!

10. WESLEY ON BOARD!

Satanic Proofs

The Internet is an incredible way for the greatest minds in academia to be in contact with each other. Although this may indeed be true, it has nothing to do with the following items pulled from the net.

Mild-Mannered Geek . . . or Satan?

The real name of "the" Bill Gates is William Henry Gates III. Nowadays he is known as Bill Gates (III), where "III" means the order of third (3rd).

By converting the letters of his current name to the ASCII values and adding his (III), you get the following:

B	**66**
I	**73**
L	**76**
L	**76**
G	**71**
A	**65**
T	**84**
E	**69**
S	**83**
+	**3**
	666

Some might ask, "How did Bill Gates get so powerful?" Coincidence? Or just the beginning of mankind's ultimate and total enslavement???

You decide!

Before you decide, consider the following:

M S - D O S 6 . 2 1

Once again, convert to ASCII values and add:

77 + 83 + 45 + 68 + 79 + 83 + 32 + 54 + 46 + 50 + 49 = 666

Once again, convert to ASCII values and add:

W I N D O W S 9 5

87 + 73 + 78 + 68 + 79 + 87 + 83 + 57 + 53 + 1 = 666

Coincidence? I think not.

Or Is Barney, the Cute Purple Dinosaur, Satan?

The Proof:

Given: Barney is a cute purple dinosaur.

Extract the Roman numerals, remembering that the Romans had no letter 'U,' and thus used 'V' instead. Thus it reads:

CVTE PVRPLE DINOSAVR

Extracting the roman numerals leaves you with: **C V V L D I V**

Add them:

100 + 5 + 5 + 50 + 500 + 1 + 5 = 666

We suspected it all along!

Bartisms Galore

The following is a collection of some of the statements young Bart has had to write on the chalkboard as punishment in the introduction to Fox Network's television show, The Simpsons.

I will not waste chalk.

I will not skateboard in the halls.

I will not burp in class.

I will not instigate revolution.

I will not draw naked ladies in class.

I did not see Elvis.

I will not call my teacher "Hot Cakes."

Garlic gum is not funny.

They are laughing at me, not with me.

I will not yell "fire" in a crowded classroom.

I will not encourage others to fly.

I will not fake my way through life.

Tar is not a plaything.

I will not Xerox my butt.

I will not trade pants with others.

I will not do that thing with my tongue.

I will not drive the principal's car.

I will not pledge allegiance to Bart.

I will not sell school property.

I will not get very far with this attitude.

I will not make flatulent noises in class.

I will not belch the national anthem.

I will not sell land in Florida.

I will not grease the monkey bars.

I will not hide behind the Fifth Amendment.

I will not do anything bad ever again.

I will not show off.

I will not sleep through my education.

I am not a dentist.

Spitwads are not free speech.

Nobody likes sunburn slappers.

High explosives and school don't mix.

I will not bribe Principal Skinner.

I will finish what I sta . . .

Hamsters cannot fly.

Underwear should be worn on the inside.

The Christmas pageant does not stink.

I will not torment the emotionally frail.

I will not carve gods.

I will not spank others.

I will not aim for the head.

I will not barf unless I'm sick.

I will not expose the ignorance of the faculty.

I saw nothing unusual in the teacher's lounge.

I will not conduct my own fire drills.

Funny noises are not funny.

I will not snap bras.

I will not fake seizures.

This punishment is not boring and meaningless.

My name is not Dr. Death.

I will not defame New Orleans.

I will not prescribe medication.

I will not bury the new kid.

I will not teach others to fly.

I will not bring sheep to class.

A burp is not an answer.

Teacher is not a leper.

I will not eat things for money.

I will not yell "She's Dead" during roll call.

The principal's toupee is not a frisbee.

I will not squeak chalk.

Goldfish don't bounce.

Mud is not one of the four food groups.

I will not skateboard in the halls.

"Bart Bucks" are not legal tender.

Why the Chicken Crossed the Road

So just why did the chicken cross the road? Here are some answers from some famous and not-so-famous people:

Aristotle: To actualize its potential.

Buddha: If you ask this question, you deny your own inner chicken self.

Caesar: To come, to see, to conquer.

Candide: To cultivate its garden.

Salvador Dali: Fish.

Darwin: It was the logical next step after coming down from the trees.

Thomas De Quincey: Because it ran out of opium.

Jacques Derrida: What is the difference? The chicken was merely deferring from one side of the road to other. And how do we get the idea of the chicken in the first place? Does it exist outside of language?

René Descartes: It crosses the road; therefore it is!

Emily Dickinson: Because it could not stop for death.

Bob Dylan: How many roads must one chicken cross?

T.S. Eliot: Do I dare to cross the road?

Ralph Waldo Emerson: It didn't cross the road; it transcended it.

Paul Erdos: It was forced to do so by the chicken-hole principle.

Michel Foucault: It did so because the discourse of crossing the road left it no choice; the police state was oppressing it.

Sigmund Freud: The chicken was obviously female and obviously interpreted the pole on which the crosswalk sign was mounted as a phallic symbol of which she was envious.

Robert Frost: To cross the road less traveled by.

Joseph Conrad: Mistah Chicken, he dead.

Johann Friedrich von Goethe: The eternal hen-principle made it do it.

Ernest Hemingway: To die. In the rain.

James Joyce: To forge in the smithy of its soul the uncreated conscience of its race.

Immanuel Kant: Because it was a duty.

Jacques Lacan: Because of its desire for object 'A.'

Gottfried Wilhelm Leibniz: In this best possible world, the road was made for it to cross.

Karl Marx: To escape the bourgeois middle-class struggle.

Gregor Mendel: To get various strains of roads.

Newton: Chickens at rest tend to stay at rest. Chickens in motion tend to cross the road.

Thomas Paine: Out of common sense.

Pyrrho the Skeptic: What road?

J. Danforth Quayle: Ite sawe ae potatoe.

Ayn Rand: It was crossing the road because of its own rational choice to do so. There cannot be a collective unconscious; desires are unique to each individual.

Georg Friedrich Riemann: The answer appears in Dirichlet's lectures.

Carl Rogers: Why do you think the chicken crossed the road?

The Sphinx: You tell me.

Margaret Thatcher: There was no alternative.

Henry David Thoreau: To live deliberately. And suck all the marrow out of life.

Mark Twain: The news of its crossing has been greatly exaggerated.

William Wordsworth: To have something to recollect in tranquillity.

Mangled Metaphors

There's a flaw in the ointment.

We'll burn that bridge when we come to it.

Don't look at me in that tone of voice.

Let's roll up our elbows and get to work.

There's no surefool way of proceeding.

Let me take you under my thumb.

That's all water over the bridge now.

That takes the cake and eats it, too.

You're treading on thin ground.

It can't hurt but help us.

Before they made him, they broke the mold.

We've got them eating out of our laps.

No sooner said, the better.

And Now, a Little Revisionist History

La Boite Bleu

Translated from the memoirs of Jean Turing-Von Neuman (a minor nineteenth-century post-Impressionist programmer)

I will never forget that spring, that day. Paris had an air of revolution. The week before, an exhibition of Seurat's listings had caused a sensation. In his unrelenting quest for simplicity, he had reduced all of programming to three machine instructions. The resulting six thousand-line bubble sort had shocked the critics.

My own recent efforts had been received poorly. I had cut and slashed through my programs, juxtaposing blocks of code in a way that exposed the underlying intensity of the algorithm without regard to convention or syntax. But it doesn't compile, they complained. As if programming was about adhering to their primitive language definitions. As if it was my duty to live within the limits of their antiquated and ordinary compilers.

So it was that day I came to La Boite Bleu seeking solace and companionship. La Boite Bleu was where we gathered those days. The wine there was cheap, the tables were large and they kept a complete set of language manuals behind the bar. As I entered, I heard Henri's measured accent above the din.

Toulouse-Lautrec was seated at a table

spread with greenbar. Manet, red-faced, loomed over him. "Damn your recursion, Henri! Iteration, however complex, is always more efficient." Manet stormed away from the table in the direction of the bar. He always seemed angry at that time. Partly because his refusal to write in anything but FORTRAN isolated him from the rest of the avant-garde, partly because people kept confusing him with Monet. Henri motioned to me to join him at the table.

He asked me if I had heard from Vincent recently. We were all concerned about van Gogh. Only a few days before he had completed an order sorting routine that required no additional memory. Unfortunately, because he had written it in C and refused, on principle, to comment his code, no one had understood a line of it. He had not taken it well.

No. Why? I replied. He and Gauguin had a violent argument last night over whether a side effect should be considered output and he hasn't been seen since. I fear he may have done something . . . rash.

We were suddenly interrupted by the waitress's terrified scream. I turned in time to see something fall from the open envelope she held in her hand. Stooping to retrieve it, I was seized by a wave of revulsion as I recognized that the object in my hand, bestially torn from its accustomed place, was the mouse from van Gogh's workstation. The waitress, who had fainted, lay in an unnoticed heap beside me. By the evening, the incident had become the talk of Paris.

The Dating Guide: What They Say Versus What They Mean

"We need to talk." — ***"I'm pregnant."***

"I had a wonderful time last night." — ***"Who the hell are you?"***

"I've been thinking a lot." — ***"You're not as attractive as when I was drunk."***

"I've learned a lot from you." — ***"Next."***

"I want a commitment." — ***"I'm sick of masturbation."***

"Did you come?" — ***"Because I didn't."***

"I have something to tell you." — ***"Get tested."***

"I'm a Romantic." — ***"I'm poor."***

"I'll give you a call." — ***"I'd rather have my nipples torn off by wild dogs than see you again."***

"I never meant to hurt you." — ***"I thought you weren't a virgin."***

"Trust me." — ***"Let's just keep this between you and me, pumpkin."***

"I love you." — ***"God, what have I gotten myself into?"***

"I think we should just be friends." — ***"You're ugly."***

"Haven't I seen you before?" — ***"Nice ass."***

"I want to make love." — ***"I want to make love."***

"Was it good for you?" — ***"I'm insecure about my manhood."***

"I think we should see other people." — ***"I have been seeing other people."***

"Let's get married." — ***"Does that mean we can do it now?"***

"We don't have to do anything until you are ready." — ***"Put out or get out."***

"I feel it's time to express our love for each other." — ***"Give me head."***

"I still think about you." — ***"I miss the sex."***

"Is there something wrong?" — ***"Is it supposed to be this soft?"***

"You're so mature." — ***"I hope you're eighteen."***

"It's never been like this before." — ***"It's my first time."***

"Yes . . . Yes . . . (scream!)." — ***"Aren't you done yet?"***

Culture Shock

An Oregonian, a Californian, and a Texan were out camping. They were lazing around a campfire when the Texan pulled out a bottle of tequila and after taking a couple of swallows, threw the bottle up in the air, pulled out his six-shooter, and neatly shot the bottle.

The Californian noted that there was still some tequila left in the bottle, but the Texan replied, "That's okay, we have plenty of tequila where I come from."

The Californian promptly brought out his bottle of white Zinfandel, took two swallows, threw it up in the air and shot it with a 9mm semiautomatic Glock pistol with a fifteen-shot clip, stating: "We have plenty of this where I come from."

The Oregonian took all this in and finally opened a bottle of hand-crafted English-style pub bitters from a Portland microbrewery. He downed the entire bottle, threw it up in the air, shot the Californian with a twelve-gauge shotgun he kept around for birds, and deftly caught the bottle.

The Texan's jaw dropped nearly to his silver buckle and his eyes widened nearly as wide as the buckle. The Oregonian, momentarily puzzled at the reaction, finally piped up: "It's okay, we have plenty of Californians where I come from, but I can get a nickel for this bottle!"

What If Dr. Seuss Did Technical Training Manuals?

Here's an easy game to play.
Here's an easy thing to say:
If a packet hits a pocket on a socket on a port,
And the bus is interrupted as a very last resort,
And the address of the memory makes your floppy disk abort,
Then the socket packet pocket has an error to report!
If your cursor finds a menu item followed by a dash,
And the double-clicking icon puts your window in the trash,
And your data is corrupted 'cause the index doesn't hash,
Then your situation's hopeless, and your system's gonna crash!
You can't say this?
What a shame, sir!
We'll find you
Another game, sir.

If the label on the cable on the table at your house,
Says the network is connected to the button on your mouse,
But your packets want to tunnel on another protocol,
That's repeatedly rejected by the printer down the hall,
And your screen is all distorted by the side effects of gauss
So your icons in the window are as wavy as a souse,
Then you may as well reboot and go out with a bang,
'Cause as sure as I'm a poet, the sucker's gonna hang!
When the copy of your floppy's getting sloppy on the disk,
And the microcode instructions cause unnecessary risk,
Then you have to flash your memory and you'll want to RAM your ROM.
Quickly turn off the computer and be sure to tell your mom!

Pirate Joke

Seems there was *a treasure ship on its way back to port. About halfway there, it was approached by a pirate, skull and crossbones waving in the breeze!*

"Captain, captain, what do we do?" asked the first mate.

"First mate," said the captain, "go to my cabin, open my sea chest, and bring me my red shirt." The first mate did so. Wearing his bright red shirt, the captain exhorted his crew to fight. So inspiring was he, in fact, that the pirate ship was repelled without casualties.

A few days later, the ship was again approached, this time by two pirate sloops!

"Captain, captain, what should we do?"

"First mate, bring me my red shirt!"

The crew, emboldened by their fearless captain, fought heroically, and managed to defeat both boarding parties, though they took many casualties. That night, the survivors had a great celebration. The first mate asked the captain the secret of his bright red shirt.

"It's simple, first mate. If I am wounded, the blood does not show, and the crew continues to fight without fear."

A week passed, and they were nearing their home port, when suddenly the lookout cried that ten ships of the enemy's armada were approaching!

"Captain, captain, we're in terrible trouble, what do we do?"

The first mate looked expectantly at the miracle worker.

Pale with fear, the captain commanded, "First mate . . . Bring me my brown pants!"

Welcome to the Army!

A line of soldiers stands in front of a huge rectangular hole in the ground. The sergeant commands: "Private Simmons!"

"Yes, sergeant?"

"Stand like this:"

```
O
_|______
| |
| |
| |
| |
| |
| |
| |
```

"Jump!!"

The soldier jumps into the hole, and the sergeant commands again:

"Private Frehley!"

"Yes, sergeant?"

"Stand like this:"

```
|
| O
\ -|-|
| |
| |
 \-\
  | |
  | |
  | |
```

"Yes, sergeant!"

"Jump!"

The soldier jumps and falls into the hole, and the sergeant commands again:

"Private Kriss!!"

"Yes, sergeant?"

"Stand like this:"

```
  | |
| |
|-| O
| | |-|
| | |
| | |
| |
| |
| |
| |
```

"Yes, sergeant!"

"Jump!"

At this point a car with a colonel arrives to that place. The colonel, very angry, comes up to the sergeant and tells him: "Sergeant, how many times do I have to tell you: Stop playing Tetris with the soldiers!"

And by That You Mean ...?

When large numbers of men are unable to find work, unemployment results.
—Calvin Coolidge

Hegel was right when he said that we learn from history that man can never learn anything from history.
—George Bernard Shaw

For those who like this sort of thing, this is the sort of thing they like.
—Abraham Lincoln

That shoe fits him like a glove.
—Anonymous

I wouldn't be paranoid if everyone didn't pick on me.
—Anonymous

People have one thing in common: they are all different.
—Anonymous

It usually takes more than three weeks to prepare a good impromptu speech.
—Mark Twain

The trouble with our times is that the future is not what it used to be.
—Paul Valéry

I must follow the people. Am I not their leader?
—Benjamin Disraeli

He lived his life to the end.
—Anonymous

You can observe a lot just by watchin'.
—Yogi Berra

The English certainly and fiercely pride themselves in never praising themselves.
—Wyndham Lewis

I am not sincere, even when I say I am not.
—Jules Renard

You've no idea of what a poor opinion I have of myself, and how little I deserve it.
—W.S. Gilbert

Hypochondria is the one disease I have not got.
—Anonymous

Inform all the troops that communications have completely broken down.
—Ashleigh Brilliant

Nobody goes to that restaurant anymore-it's too crowded.
—Anonymous

Just the omission of Jane Austen's books alone would make a fairly good library out of a library that hadn't a book in it.
—Mark Twain

A hospital is no place to be sick.

Our comedies are not to be laughed at.

I can give you a definite perhaps.

The Internet's List of Samuel Goldwynisms

Samuel Goldwyn, when told a script was full of old clichés: "Let's have some new clichés."

Gentlemen, include me out.

A verbal contract isn't worth the paper it's printed on.

I can tell you in two words: im possible.

Samuel Goldwyn, on being told that a friend had named his son Sam, after him: "Why did you do that? Every Tom, Dick, and Harry is named Sam!"

I paid too much for it, but it's worth it.

Gentlemen, for your information, I have a question to ask you.

I read part of it all the way through.

If I could drop dead right now, I'd be the happiest man alive.

I never put on a pair of shoes until I've worn them at least five years.

Let's bring it up to date with some snappy nineteenth-century dialogue.

Samuel Goldwyn: What kind of dancing does Martha Graham do?
Associate: Modern dancing.
Samuel Goldwyn: I don't want her then, modern dancing is so old-fashioned.

I don't think anyone should write their autobiography until after they're dead.

Anyone who goes to a psychiatrist ought to have his head examined.

(On a film set of a tenement)
Goldwyn: Why is everything so dirty here?
Director: Because it's supposed to be a slum area.
Goldwyn: Well, this slum cost a lot of money. It should look better than an ordinary slum.

Gentlemen, listen to me slowly.

That's the trouble with directors—always biting the hand that lays the golden egg.

Keep a stiff upper chin.

We can get the Indians from the reservoir.

(In discussing Lillian Hellman's play, The Children's Hour*)*
Goldwyn: Maybe we ought to buy it?
Associate: Forget it, Mr. Goldwyn, it's about lesbians.
Goldwyn: That's okay, we'll make them Americans.

Don't worry about the war. It's all over but the shooting.

Associate: It's too caustic for film.
Goldwyn: To hell with the cost, if it's a good story, I'll make it.

Here Are Some Questions That Make You Want to Ask . . . Why?

If nothing ever sticks to Teflon, how do they make Teflon stick to the pan?

Do you need a silencer if you are going to shoot a mime?

Have you ever imagined a world with no hypothetical situations?

How does the guy who drives the snowplow get to work in the mornings?

If 7-11 is open twenty-four hours a day, 365 days a year, why are there locks on the doors?

If a cow laughed real hard, would milk come out her nose?

If you tied buttered toast to the back of a cat and dropped it from a height, what would happen?

Why isn't "phonetic" spelled the way it sounds?

Why are there interstate highways in Hawaii?

Why are there flotation devices under plane seats instead of parachutes?

Why are cigarettes sold in gas stations when smoking is prohibited there?

Why do "fat chance" and "slim chance" mean the same thing?

If you can't drink and drive, why do you need a driver's license to buy liquor, and why do bars have parking lots?

Why do they put Braille dots on the keypad of the drive-up ATM?

Why do we drive on parkways and park on driveways?

Why isn't "palindrome" spelled the same way backwards?

Why did kamikaze pilots wear helmets?

Why is it that when you transport something by car, it's called a "shipment," but when you transport something by ship, it's called "cargo?"

Why is it that when you're driving and looking for an address, you turn down the volume on the radio?

If you have your finger touching the rearview mirror that says "objects in mirror are closer than they appear," how can that be possible?

Why is it so hard to remember how to spell "mnemonic?"

If someone invented instant water, what would they mix it with?

Why is it called a TV "set" when you only get one?

Why does your nose "run" and your feet "smell"?

Why does an alarm clock "go off" when it begins ringing?

If pro is the opposite of con, is progress the opposite of congress?

Why does "cleave" mean both split apart and stick together?

Why is it, whether you sit up or sit down, the result is the same?

Why is it called a "building" when it is already built?

Why do they call them "apartments" when they are all stuck together?

Why is there an expiration date on sour cream?

Why do "flammable" and "inflammable" mean the same thing?

How can someone "draw a blank"?

Shouldn't there be a shorter word for "monosyllabic"?

Why is the word "abbreviate" so long?

What is another word for "thesaurus"?

If 75 percent of all accidents happen within five miles of home, why not move ten miles away?

Why doesn't "onomatopoeia" sound like what it is?

When they ship Styrofoam, what do they pack it in?

Need Abuse?

A great source of information, the Internet can also provide you with personalized insults, courtesy of these two sites. You get a new insult each time you visit. For your convenience, we've gathered a few.

Enter the Abuse-A-Tron!

You seduce family pets, you fat, barf-smelling, ad agency rep-buggering, discognizant heir of an optimistic fatalist.

You chase cars and bark at them, you contaminated, worm-scarfing, llama-exploiting, sedentary sire of Barney the Dinosaur.

You smell of elderberries, you boot-licking, worm-eating, mutant turtle-buggering, carpet-bagging whelp of an entomologist with carnal knowledge of cockroaches.

Or . . .

At the request of John Doe, the Shakespearean Insult Service (http://kite.ithaca.ny.us/insult.html) has generated this semipersonalized, random insult in the tone of the Bard, especially for you.

"Thou art a craven pottle-deep toad-spotted skainsmate, Scott."

Politically Correct Terms

Dirty Old Man: Sexually focused chronologically gifted individual.

Perverted: Sexually dysfunctional.

Panhandler: Unaffiliated applicant for private-sector funding.

Serial Killer: Person with difficult-to-meet needs.

Lazy: Motivationally deficient.

Fail: Achieve a deficiency.

Dishonest: Ethically disoriented.

Bald: Follicularly challenged.

Clumsy: Uniquely coordinated.

Body Odor: Nondiscretionary fragrance.

Alive: Temporarily metabolically abled.

Worst: Least best.

Wrong: Differently logical.

Ugly: Cosmetically different.

Unemployed: Involuntarily leisured.

Short: Vertically challenged.

Dead: Living impaired.

Vagrant: Nonspecifically destinationed individual.

Spendthrift: Negative saver.

Stoned: Chemically inconvenienced.

Pregnant: Parasitically oppressed.

Ignorant: Knowledge-based nonpossessor.

The Ten Best Elf Pickup Lines

1. *"I'm down here!"*
2. *"Just because I've got bells on my feet doesn't mean I'm a sissy!"*
3. *"I was a lawn ornament for Gary Sweet."*
4. *"I can get you off the naughty list!"*
5. *"I have certain needs that can't be satisfied by working on toys."*
6. *"I'm a magical being! Take off your bra!"*
7. *"It's not size that matters, babe!"*
8. *"I get a thimbleful of tequila into me and I turn into a wild man!"*
9. *"You'd look hot in a Raggedy Ann wig!"*
10. *"I can eat my weight in cocktail frankfurters!"*

Things Not to Say or Do at Your Thesis Defense

1. "Ladies and Gentlemen, please rise for the singing of our National Anthem . . ."
2. Charge 25 cents a cup for coffee.
3. "Charge the mound" when a professor beans you with a high, fast question.
4. Describe parts of your thesis using interpretive dance.
5. Lead the spectators in a Wave.
6. "Okay—which one of you farted?"
7. "Anybody else as drunk as I am?"
8. "You call that a question? How the hell did they make you a professor?"
9. "Ladies and gentlemen, as I dim the lights, please hold hands and concentrate so that we may channel the spirit of Lord Kelvin . . ."
10. Have bodyguards outside the room to "discourage" certain professors from sitting in.
11. Puppet show.
12. Animal sacrifice to the god of the Underworld.
13. Have a bikini-clad model be in charge of changing the overheads.
14. Group prayer.

15. "And it would have worked if it weren't for those meddling kids . . ."
16. Charge a cover and check for ID.
17. Door prizes and a raffle.
18. Two-drink minimum.
19. "And now a reading from the Book of Mormon . . ."
20. "Professor Robinson, will you marry me?"
21. Have a sing-along.
22. Hang a piñata over the table and have a strolling mariachi band.
23. "I'm sorry, Professor Smith, I didn't say Simon says any questions?"
24. "I could answer that, but then I'd have to kill you."
25. "Everybody rhumba!"

Written by Master Peter Dutton; contributions by Jim Lalopoulos, Alison Berube, Jeff Cohen, Patricia Whitson, and a few others.

You all know about the Darwin Award—it's an annual honor given to the person who did the gene pool the biggest service by killing themselves in the most extraordinarily stupid way.

"Darwin Award" Nominee:

Last year's winner was the fellow who was killed by a soft-drink machine that toppled over on top of him as he was attempting to tip a free soda out of it.

The Arizona (U.S.) Highway Patrol came upon a pile of smoldering metal embedded into the side of a cliff rising above the road, at the apex of a curve.

The wreckage resembled the site of an airplane crash, but it was a car. The type of car was unidentifiable at the scene.

The boys in the lab finally figured out what it was, and what had happened. It seems that a guy had somehow got hold of a JATO unit (Jet Assisted Take Off, actually a solid-fuel rocket) that is used to give heavy military transport planes an extra "push" for taking off from short airfields. He had driven his Chevy Impala out into the desert, and found a long, straight stretch of road. Then he attached the JATO unit to his car, jumped in, got up some speed, and fired off the JATO!!

Best as they could determine, he was

doing somewhere between 250 and 300 mph (350–420 kph) when he came to that curve. The brakes were completely burned away, apparently from trying to slow the car.

Note: Solid-fuel rockets don't have an "off." Once started, they burn at full thrust until the fuel is all gone.

New Element Discovered at Naval Research Lab

The heaviest element known to science was recently discovered by physicists at the Naval Research Laboratory. The element, tentatively named Administratium, has no protons or electrons, and thus has an atomic number of 0. However, it does have 1 neutron, 126 assistant neutrons, 75 vice neutrons and 111 assistant vice neutrons. This gives it an atomic mass of 312.

These 312 particles are held together in a nucleus by a force that involves the continuous exchange of mesonlike particles called "morons." Since it has no electrons, Administratium is inert. However, it can be detected chemically as it impedes every reaction it comes in contact with. According to the discoverers, a minute amount of Administratium caused one reaction to take over four days to complete, when it would normally occur in less than one second.

Administratium has a normal half-life of approximately three years, at which time it does not actually decay, but instead undergoes a reorganization in which assistant neutrons, vice neutrons, and assistant vice neutrons exchange places. Some studies have shown that the atomic weight actually increases after such reorganization.

Research at other laboratories indicates that Administratium occurs naturally in the atmosphere. It tends to concentrate at certain points such as government agencies, large corporations, and universities, and can even be found in the newest, best-maintained buildings. Scientists point out that Administratium is known to be toxic at any level of concentration and can easily destroy any productive reactions where it is allowed to accumulate. Attempts are being made to determine how Administratium can be controlled to prevent irreversible damage, but results are not promising.

The Ten Best Uses for Data's Detached Head

1. *Hood ornament for shuttle craft.*
2. *Replace Troi's broken Chia pet.*
3. *Prop open doors for maintenance crews.*
4. *Lawn decoration in arboretum.*
5. *Footstool for captain's chair.*
6. *Combination paperweight/stapler for Picard's desk.*
7. *Decorative air filter in Picard's fish tank.*
8. *Keep Worf's coffee table from shaking.*
9. *Trade to Ferengi for Star Trek hologram cards.*
10. *Two words: tether ball.*

Net signatures are the short phrases people attach to the end of their E-mail messages.

The Best Net Signatures

Warning: Dates in calendar are closer than they appear.

Daddy, why doesn't this magnet pick up this floppy disk?

Give me ambiguity or give me something else.

We are born naked, wet, and hungry. Then things get worse.

Pentiums melt in your PC, not in your hand.

Suicidal twin kills sister by mistake!

Did anyone see my lost carrier?

Make it idiot-proof and someone will make a better idiot.

I'm not a complete idiot, some parts are missing!

Always remember you're unique, just like everyone else.

A flashlight is a case for holding dead batteries.

Lottery: A tax on people who are bad at math.

There's too much blood in my caffeine system.

Artificial Intelligence usually beats real stupidity.

Hard work has a future payoff. Laziness pays off now.

Friends help you move. Real friends help you move bodies.

Ever notice how fast Windows runs? Neither did I.

Double your drive space—delete Windows!

What is a "free" gift? Aren't all gifts free?

If ignorance is bliss, you must be orgasmic.

"Very funny, Scotty. Now beam down my clothes."

Consciousness: That annoying time between naps.

Oops. My brain just hit a bad sector.

I used to have a handle on life, then it broke.

I don't suffer from insanity. I enjoy every minute of it.

Better to understand a little than to misunderstand a lot.

The gene pool could use a little chlorine.

When there's a will, I want to be in it.

Okay, who put a "stop payment" on my reality check?

Few women admit their age. Few men act theirs.

I'm as confused as a baby in a topless bar.

We have enough youth, how about a fountain of smart?

All generalizations are false, including this one.

Change is inevitable, except from a vending machine.

"Criminal Lawyer" is a redundancy.

Macs vs. IBMs

As I was walking down the street the other day, I noticed a man working on his house. He seemed to be having a lot of trouble. As I came closer, I saw that he was trying to pound a nail into a board by a window—with his forehead. He seemed to be in a great deal of pain. This made me feel very bad, watching him suffer so much just to fix his windowpane. I thought to myself, "Here is an opportunity to make someone very happy simply by showing him a better way to do things." Seeing him happy would make me happy too. So I said, "Excuse me sir, there is a better way to do that."

He stopped pounding his head on the nail and with blood streaming down his face said, "What?"

I said, "There is a better way to pound that nail. You can use a hammer."

He said, "What?"

I said "A hammer. It's a heavy piece of metal on a stick. You can use it to pound the nail. It's faster and it doesn't hurt when you use it."

"A hammer, huh?"

"That's right. If you get one I can show you how to use it and you'll be amazed how much easier it will make your job."

Somewhat bewildered, he said, "I think I have seen hammers, but I thought they were just toys for kids."

"Well, I suppose kids could play with

hammers, but I think what you saw were brightly colored plastic hammers. They look a bit like real hammers, but they are much cheaper and don't really do anything," I explained.

"Oh," he said. "But hammers are more expensive than using my forehead. I don't want to spend the money for a hammer."

Somewhat frustrated I said, "But in the long run the hammer would pay for itself because you would spend more time pounding nails and less time treating head wounds."

"But I can't do as much with a hammer as I can with my forehead," he said with conviction.

Exasperated, I went on. "Well, I'm not quite sure what else you've been using your forehead for, but hammers are marvelously useful tools. You can pound nails, pull nails, pry apart boards. In fact every day people like you seem to be finding new ways to use hammers. I'm sure a hammer would do all these things much better than your forehead."

"But why should I start using a hammer? All my friends pound nails with their foreheads, too. If there were a better way to do it I'm sure one of them would have told me," he countered.

He had caught me off guard. "Perhaps they are all thinking the same thing—you could be the first one to discover this new way to do things," I said with enthusiasm.

With a skeptical look in his blood-stained eye he said, "Look, some of my friends are professional carpenters. You can't tell me they don't know the best way to pound nails."

"Well, even professionals become set in their ways and resist change." Then in a frustrated yell I continued, "I mean, come on! You can't just sit there and try to convince me that using your forehead to pound nails is better than using a hammer!"

He yelled back, "Hey listen, buddy, I've been pounding nails with my forehead for many years now. Sure, it was painful at first, but now it's second nature to me. Besides, all my friends do it this way, and the only people I've ever seen using hammers were little kids. So take your stupid little children's toys and get the hell off my property."

Stunned, I started to step back. I nearly tripped over a large box of head bandages. I noticed a very expensive price tag on the box and an eerie blue company logo on the price tag. I had seen all I needed to see. This man had somehow been brainwashed, probably by the expensive bandage company, and was beyond help. Hell, let him bleed, I thought. People like that deserve to bleed to death.

I walked along, happy that I owned not one but three hammers at home. I used them every day at school, and I use them now every day at work and I love them. A sharp pain hit my stomach as I recalled the days before I used hammers, but I reconciled myself with the thought that tonight at the hammer users club meeting I could talk to all my friends about their hammers. We will make jokes about all the idiots we know that don't have hammers and discuss whether we should spend all of our money buying the fancy new hammers that just came out. Then when I get home, like every night, I will sit up and use one of my hammers until very late when I finally fall asleep. In the morning I will wake up ready to go out into the world proclaiming to all nonhammer users how they too could become an expert hammer user like me.

Actual Newspaper Headlines

Something Went Wrong in Jet Crash, Expert Says

Police Begin Campaign to Run Down Jaywalkers

Safety Experts Say School Bus Passengers Should Be Belted

Drunk Gets Nine Months in Violin Case

Farmer Bill Dies in House

Iraqi Head Seeks Arms

Is There a Ring of Debris Around Uranus?

Stud Tires Out

Prostitutes Appeal to Pope

Panda Mating Fails; Veterinarian Takes Over

Soviet Virgin Lands Short of Goal Again

British Left Waffles on Falkland Islands

Eye Drops Off Shelf

Teacher Strikes Idle Kids

Reagan Wins on Budget, But More Lies Ahead

Squad Helps Dog Bite Victim

Shot Off Woman's Leg Helps Nicklaus to 66

Enraged Cow Injures House

Miners Refuse to Work After Death

Juvenile Court to Try Shooting Defendant

Stolen Painting Found by Tree

Two Soviet Ships Collide, One Dies

Two Sisters Reunited After Eighteen Years in Checkout Counter

Killer Sentenced to Die for Second Time in Ten Years

Never Withhold Herpes Infection from Loved One

Drunken Drivers Paid $1,000 In '84

War Dims Hope for Peace

If Strike Isn't Settled Quickly, It May Last a While

Cold Wave Linked to Temperatures

Enfiels Couple Slain; Police Suspect Homicide

Important Breaking Sesame Street News!

11/17 2:55 EDT V055

New York (AP)—**Big Bird**, the famed friendly muppet of Sesame Street, has apparently gone on a rampage. Several Muppets are known to be dead, including Prairie Dawn, Oscar the Grouch, and Bert—longtime friend, roommate, and occasional lover of Ernie. The bird is now reportedly holding Maria hostage in a five-floor tenement near Hooper's Store. New York City Police SWAT teams have surrounded the building.

11/17 4:26 EDT V743

New York (AP)—**Big Bird**, Sesame Street Muppet, is reported dead at this hour after an hour-and-a-half hostage standoff with New York City Police. Kermit the Frog, Sesame Street Muppet on the scene, reports that as police stormed the five-story tenement building where the bird was holding Maria hostage, Big Bird flew out an upper-story window at them in a Kamikazelike attack. Police SWAT units brought down the bird in a hail of automatic weapons fire. Dead are: Prairie Dawn, Oscar the Grouch, Bert, and Big Bird. There is no information available concerning Maria.

11/17 8:47 EDT V246

NEW YORK (AP)—**The Professor** and his assistant, Beaker, Muppet chemists, have reportedly found angel dust in Big Bird's feed. Big Bird was killed by police early this morning after the bird went on a killing spree on Sesame Street. Maria, taken hostage during the ordeal, has survived unharmed. Three Muppets were killed by the bird: Prairie Dawn (a friendly, pig-tailed Muppet girl-child), Oscar the Grouch (a green garbage can–dwelling grumpy Muppet), and Bert (the famous gay paper clip collector and pigeon friend). Authorities in the area report that the bad seed was purchased at the local Hooper's.

11/17 11:15 EDT V543

NEW YORK(AP)—**Police are asking** all motorists and humans to stay away from Sesame Street today as tensions are running high among the Muppets. Many reportedly are outraged at the tainted food supply and at how the police handled the hostage situation. According to bystanders on the scene at the time, Mr. Snuffalupagus pleaded with police to be allowed to talk Big Bird down. Instead, police stormed the building with deadly results. Ernie is said to be despondent at the loss of his good buddy Bert.

11/17 17:25 EDT V927

NEW YORK (AP)—**Violence erupted** again on Sesame Street at five o'clock this afternoon. As thousands of humans driving home took a sightseeing tour of the scene of Big Bird's deadly rampage, Muppets became enraged. Hundreds of Muppets, large and small, stalked the streets and surrounded humans in their cars. In at least one case, ten Muppets pulled a motorist from his car and beat him with large Styrofoam letters. Police again arrived on the scene in force. At this hour, quiet is restored—but tensions are very high.

This is an actual essay that a guy used to get himself accepted at NYU two or three years ago. The author of this essay, Hugh Gallagher, now attends NYU.

So You Say You Want to Go to College?

In order for the admissions staff of our college to get to know you, the applicant, better, we ask that you answer the following question: are there any significant experiences you have had, or accomplishments you have realized, that have helped to define you as a person?

I am a dynamic figure, often seen scaling walls and crushing ice. I have been known to remodel train stations on my lunch breaks, making them more efficient in the area of heat retention. I translate ethnic slurs for Cuban refugees, I write award-winning operas, I manage time efficiently. Occasionally, I tread water for three days in a row. I woo women with my sensuous and godlike trombone playing, I can pilot bicycles up severe inclines with unflagging speed, and I cook thirty-minute brownies in twenty minutes. I am an expert in stucco, a veteran in love, and an outlaw in Peru.

Using only a hoe and a large glass of water, I once single-handedly defended a small village in the Amazon Basin from a horde of ferocious army ants. I play bluegrass cello, I was scouted by the Mets, I am the subject of numerous documentaries. When I'm bored, I build large suspension bridges in my yard. I enjoy urban hang gliding. On Wednesdays, after school, I repair electrical appliances free of charge.

I am an abstract artist, a concrete analyst, and a ruthless bookie. Critics worldwide swoon over my original line of corduroy evening wear. I don't perspire. I am a private citizen, yet I receive fan mail. I have been caller number nine and have won the weekend passes. Last summer I toured New Jersey with a traveling centrifugal-force demonstration. I bat .400. My deft floral arrangements have earned me fame in international botany circles. Children trust me.

I can hurl tennis rackets at small moving objects with deadly accuracy. I once read *Paradise Lost, Moby-Dick,* and *David Copperfield* in one day and still had time to refurbish an entire dining room that evening. I know the exact location of every food item in the supermarket. I have performed several covert operations for the CIA. I sleep once a week; when I do sleep, I sleep in a chair. While on vacation in Canada, I successfully negotiated with a group of terrorists who had seized a small bakery. The laws of physics do not apply to me.

I balance, I weave, I dodge, I frolic, and

my bills are all paid. On weekends, to let off steam, I participate in full-contact origami. Years ago I discovered the meaning of life but forgot to write it down. I have made extraordinary four-course meals using only a Mouli and a toaster oven. I breed prize-winning clams. I have won bullfights in San Juan, cliff-diving competitions in Sri Lanka, and spelling bees at the Kremlin. I have played *Hamlet,* I have performed open-heart surgery, and I have spoken with Elvis.

But I have not yet gone to college.

The Book of Creation

Chapter 1

1. In the beginning God created Dates.

2. And the date was Monday, July 4, 4004 B.C.

3. And God said, let there be light; and there was light. And when there was Light, God saw the Date, that it was Monday, and he got down to work; for verily, he had a Big Job to do.

4. And God made pottery shards and Silurian mollusks and pre-Cambrian limestone strata; and flints and Jurassic mastodon tusks and Picanthropus erectus skulls and Cretaceous placentals made he; and those cave paintings at Lascaux. And that was that, for the first workday.

5. And God saw that he had made many wondrous things, but that he had not wherein to put it all. And God said, Let the heavens be divided from the earth; and let us bury all of these Things which we have made in the earth; but not too deep.

6. And God buried all the Things which he had made, and that was that.

7. And the morning and the evening and the overtime were Tuesday.

8. And God said, Let there be water; and let the dry land appear; and that was that.

9. And God called the dry land Real Estate; and the water called he the Sea. And

in the land and beneath it put he crude oil, grades one through six; and natural gas put he thereunder, and prehistoric carboniferous forests yielding anthracite and other ligneous matter; and all these called he Resources; and he made them Abundant.

10. And likewise all that was in the sea, even unto two hundred miles from the dry land, called he resources; all that was therein, like manganese nodules, for instance.

11. And the morning unto the evening had been a long day; which he called Wednesday.

12. And God said, Let the earth bring forth abundantly every moving creature I can think of, with or without backbones, with or without wings or feet, or fins or claws, vestigial limbs and all, right now; and let each one be of a separate species. For lo, I can make whatsoever I like, whensoever I like.

13. And the earth brought forth abundantly all creatures, great and small, with and without backbones, with and without wings and feet and fins and claws, vestigial limbs and all, from bugs to brontosauruses.

14. But God blessed them all, saying, Be fruitful and multiply and Evolve Not.

15. And God looked upon the species he hath made, and saw that the earth was exceedingly crowded, and he said unto

them, Let each species compete for what it needed; for Healthy Competition is My Law. And the species competeth amongst themselves, the cattle and the creeping things; and some madeth it and some didn't; and the dogs ate the dinosaurs and God was pleased.

16. And God took the bones from the dinosaurs, and caused them to appear mighty old; and cast he them about the land and the sea. And he took every tiny creature that had not madeth it, and caused them to become fossils; and cast he them about likewise.

17. And just to put matters beyond the valley of the shadow of a doubt God created carbon dating. And this is the origin of species.

18. And in the Evening of the day which was Thursday, God saw that he had put in another good day's work.

19. And God said, Let us make man in our image, after our likeness, which is tall and well-formed and pale of hue: and let us also make monkeys, which resembleth us not in any wise, but are short and ill-formed and hairy. And God added, Let man have dominion over the monkeys and the fowl of the air and every species, endangered or otherwise.

20. So God created Man in His own image; tall and well-formed and pale of

hue created He him, and nothing at all like the monkeys.

21. And God said, Behold I have given you every herb bearing seed, which is upon the face of the earth. But ye shalt not smoketh it, lest it giveth you ideas.

22. And to every beast of the earth and every fowl of the air I have given also every green herb, and to them it shall be for meat. But they shall be for you. And the Lord God your Host suggesteth that the flesh of cattle goeth well with that of the fin and the claw; thus shall Surf be wedded unto Turf.

23. And God saw everything he had made, and he saw that it was very good; and God said, It just goes to show Me what the private sector can accomplish. With a lot of fool regulations this could have taken billions of years.

24. And the evening of the fifth day, which had been the roughest day yet, God said, Thank me it's Friday. And God made the weekend.

Chapter 2

1. Thus the heavens and the earth were finished, and all in five days, and all less than six thousand years ago; and if thou believest it not, in a sling shalt thou find thy hindermost quarters.

2. Likewise God took the dust of the ground, and the slime of the Sea and the

scum of the earth and formed Man therefrom; and breathed the breath of life right in his face. And he became Free to Choose.

3. And God made a Marketplace eastward of Eden, in which the man was free to play. And this was the Free Play of the Marketplace.

4. And out of the ground made the LORD God to grow four trees: the Tree of Life, and the Liberty Tree, and the Pursuit of Happiness Tree, and the Tree of the Knowledge of Sex.

5. And the LORD God commanded the man, saying, This is my Law, which is called the Law of Supply and Demand. Investeth thou in the trees of Life, Liberty, and the Pursuit of Happiness, and thou shalt make for thyself a fortune. For what fruit thou eatest not, that thou mayest sell, and with the seeds thereof expand thy operations.

6. But the fruit of the tree of the Knowledge of Sex, thou mayest not eat; nor mayest thou invest therein, nor profit thereby nor expand its operations; for that is a mighty waste of seed.

7. And the man was exceeding glad. But he asked the LORD God: Who then shall labor in this Marketplace? For I am not management, being tall and well-formed and pale of hue?

8. And the LORD God said unto himself, Verily, this kid hath the potential which is Executive.

9. And out of the ground the LORD God formed every beast of the field and every fowl of the air, and brought them unto Adam to labor for him. And they labored for peanuts.

10. Then Adam was again exceeding glad. But he spake once more unto the LORD God, saying, Lo, I am free to play in the Marketplace of the LORD, and have cheap labor in plenty; but to whom shall I sell my surplus fruit and realize a fortune thereby?

11. And the LORD God said unto himself, Verily, this is a Live One.

12. And he caused a deep sleep to fall upon Adam and he took from him one of his ribs, which was a spare rib.

13. And the spare rib which the LORD God had taken from the man, made he woman. And he brought her unto the man, saying:

14. This is Woman and she shall purchase your fruit; and ye shall realize a fortune thereby. For Man produceth and Woman consumeth, wherefore she shall be called the consumer.

15. And they were both decently clad, the Man and the Woman, from the neck even unto the ankles, so they were not ashamed.

Chapter 3

1. Now the snake in the grass was more permissive than any beast of the field which

the LORD God had made. And he said unto the woman, Why has thou accepted this lowly and submissive role? For art thou not human, even as the man is human?

2. And the woman said unto the snake in the grass, the LORD God hath ordained that I am placed under the man, and must do whatsoever he telleth me to do; for is he not the Man?

3. But the snake in the grass laughed a cunning laugh, and said unto the woman, Is it not right and just that thou shouldst fulfill thy potential? For art thou not comely in thy flesh, even as the man is comely in his flesh?

4. And the woman said, Nay, I know not, for hath not the LORD God clad us decently, from the neck even unto the ankles; and forbidden that we eat of the Tree of the Knowledge of Sex?

5. But the snake in the grass said unto the woman, whispering even into her very ear, saying, Whatsoever feeleth good, do thou it; and believeth thou me, it feeleth good.

6. And when the woman saw the fruit of the Tree of the Knowledge of Sex, that it was firm and plump and juicy, she plucked thereof, and sank her teeth therein, and gave also to her husband, and he likewise sank his teeth therein.

7. And the eyes of both of them were opened, and they saw that they were not naked.

8. And the woman loosened then Adam's uppermost garment, and he likewise loosened hers; and she loosened his nethermost garment, and the man then loosened her nethermost garment; until they were out of their garments both, and likewise of their minds.

9. And, lo! they did dance upon the grass of the ground, and they did rock backward, and roll forward continually.

10. And as they did rock and roll, the serpent that was cunning did play upon a stringed instrument of music, and did smite his tail upon the ground in a hypnotic rhythm, and he did sing in a voice that was like unto four voices: She loveth you, yea, yea, yea.

11. And they did both twist and shout, and fall into a frenzy, both the man and the woman, and lay themselves upon the ground, and commit there abominations.

12. And when they were spent from their abominations, they did take the herb bearing seed, and did roll it and smoke it; and lo! it gaveth them ideas, even as the LORD God had said; and they were like to commit new abominations.

13. Now the LORD God was walking in the garden in the cool of the day, with his dog; and as Adam and his wife were beginning these new abominations, the LORD God did stub the toe of his foot upon their hindermost quarters.

14. And the LORD God waxed wroth, and said unto Adam, Wherefore art thou naked? And what is that thou smokest? And why art thou not at thy work? For have I not said that it is the man's part to produce, and the part of the woman to consume whatever he produceth?

15. And Adam and his wife did look upon one another, and did giggle.

16. Whereupon the LORD God waxed exceeding wroth, and he said, Hast thou eaten of the tree, whereof I commanded thee that thou shouldst not eat?

17. And the man said, The woman whom you gavest to be with me made me do it.

18. And the LORD God said unto the woman, What is this that thou has done? And the woman said, The snake in the grass made me do it.

19. And the snake in the grass said, The devil made me do it.

20. And the LORD God said unto the snake in the grass, Thou art a permissive beast; wherefore art thou cursed to crawl upon thy belly, and be made into belts and boots and handbags hereafter.

21. Unto the woman He said, Since thou has harkened unto the snake in the grass which is broad-of-mind and permissive; henceforth let it be thy lot to be confused and scattered in thy brains, and to be plagued by demons who shall tempt thee to become that which thou canst not be: such as a warrior, or an extin-

guisher of fires, or an operator of heavy machinery.

22. And since thou has put aside the decent clothing wherein I clad thee, hereafter no garment shall satisfy thee, and thou shalt be overcome by longings to change thy raiment every spring and fall.

23. And above all this, since thou hast desired to taste of the fruit of the Tree of the Knowledge of Sex, now let thy very body be a curse unto thee. From generation unto generation, men shalt whistle and hoot after thee as thou passest; yea, and women also.

24. And unto Adam he said, Woe unto thee who hast harkened not to the voice of the LORD thy God, but rather to her who is thy inferior; for thou wast free to choose. Now shalt thou be banished from the Marketplace and the Free Play thereof; neither shalt thou pluck the fruit from the Trees of Life and Liberty and the Pursuit of Happiness.

25. In the sweat of thy face shalt thou earn thy bread, and bankruptcy shall be thy lot; and upon thy back, as a burden unto thee, thou shalt bear Big Government; for thou has sinned.

26. And the LORD God said unto the man, Behold, thy knowledge of sex shall be as a curse upon thee and thy generations; and thy loins shall be a trial to thee.

27. For whensoever thou goest into a public place, then shall thy member rise up; when thou sitteth to eat and drink

among thy fellows, likewise shall it rise up; yea, even when thou standeth before the people to preach unto them in my name, shall it rise up, and be a scandal unto thee, and make an unseemly lump in thy garments; yet when thou goest into thy wife shall thy member wither, and rise up not.

And then the LORD God was silent, and waxed sad, and made as if to leave them there. But he turned and spoke softly unto Adam and his wife Eve, saying, Knowest thou something? Mine only hope is this: *That someday, ye have children who do unto you the way ye have done unto me.*

After the Flood: A Mathematician's View

The ark lands after the Flood. Noah lets all the animals out. Says, "Go and multiply." Several months pass. Noah decides to check up on the animals. All are doing fine except a pair of snakes. "What's the problem?" says Noah. "Cut down some trees and let us live there," say the snakes. Noah follows their advice. Several more weeks pass. Noah checks on the snakes again. Lots of little snakes, everybody is happy. Noah asks, "Want to tell me how the trees helped?"

"Certainly," say the snakes.

"We're adders, and we need logs to multiply."

You Can Tell It's Going to Be a Rotten Day When ...

You wake up facedown on the pavement.

You put your bra on backward and it fits better.

You call suicide prevention and they put you on hold.

You see a *60 Minutes* news team waiting in your office.

You want to put on the clothes you wore home from the party and they aren't there.

You turn on the news and they're showing emergency routes out of the city.

You wake up to discover your waterbed has broken, then remember you don't have a waterbed.

Your car horn goes off accidentally and remains stuck as you follow a group of Hell's Angels down the motorway.

Your wife wakes up feeling amorous and you have a headache.

Your boss tells you not to bother taking off your coat.

You wake up and your braces are locked together.

You call your answering service and they tell you it's none of your business.

Your blind date turns out to be your ex-wife.

Your income tax return check bounces.

You put both contact lenses in the same eye.

Your pet rock snaps at you.

Your wife says, "Good morning, Bill" and your name is George.

—Author unknown . . . but troubled.

Twenty Surefire Signs That Star Trek Is Taking Over Your Life:

1. Saying "Make it so" in casual conversation.
2. Indignation that the periodic table doesn't include dilithium and tritanium.
3. Able to use "variable phase inverter" in a sentence without excessive thought first.
4. More than one pair of Spock's ears in a junk drawer.
5. You've figured out the Star Date system.
6. Sudden urge to wear lots of Lycra.
7. Scanning the shelves at local liquor stores for synthehol.
8. The *Star Trek* theme becomes background music in your dreams.
9. Major quote sources for thesis are Shakespeare, the Bible, and "The Omega Glory."
10. Memorization of the crew's authorization numbers.

11. Forgetting that today's elevators don't have voice interface.
12. Attending a convention wearing non-Terran vestments.
13. Actual serious thoughts about buying that three-hundred-dollar model of the *Enterprise* from the Franklin Mint.
14. Understanding Klingon.
15. Lecturing any science professor on how transporters work.
16. Playing fizzbin and understanding it.
17. "The Outrageous Okona" seems like a fine piece of writing and dramatic stylistics.
18. Paying rapt attention during those endless special effects sequences in *ST:TNG*.
19. Inexplicable rock-climbing urges.
20. More than three original episode outlines buried in your drawers.

College Religion

THE DEAN

Leaps tall buildings in a single bound
Is more powerful than a locomotive
Is faster than a speeding bullet
Walks on water
Gives policy to God

THE DEPARTMENT HEAD

Leaps short buildings in a single bound
Is more powerful than a switch engine
Is just as fast as a speeding bullet
Talks with God

PROFESSOR

Leaps short buildings with a running start and favorable winds
Is almost as powerful as a switch engine
Is faster than a speeding BB
Walks on water in an indoor swimming pool
Talks with God if a special request is honored

ASSOCIATE PROFESSOR

Barely clears a Quonset hut
Loses tug-of-war with a locomotive
Can fire a speeding bullet
Swims well
Is occasionally addressed by God

ASSISTANT PROFESSOR

Makes high marks on the walls when trying to leap tall buildings
Is run over by locomotives
Can sometimes handle a gun without inflicting self-injury

Treads water
Talks to animals

INSTRUCTOR

Climbs walls continually
Rides the rails
Plays Russian roulette
Walks on thin ice
Prays a lot

GRADUATE STUDENT

Runs into buildings
Recognizes locomotives two out of three times
Is not issued ammunition
Can stay afloat with a life jacket
Talks to walls

UNDERGRADUATE STUDENT

Falls over doorstep when trying to enter buildings
Says "Look at the choo-choo"
Wets himself with a water pistol
Plays in mud puddles
Mumbles to himself

DEPARTMENT SECRETARY

Lifts buildings and walks under them
Kicks locomotives off the tracks
Catches speeding bullets in her teeth and eats them
Freezes water with a single glance
Is God.

Job Security

Three scientists (an engineer, a physicist, and a mathematician) are staying in a hotel while attending a technical seminar. The engineer wakes up and smells smoke. He goes out into the hallway and sees a fire, so he fills a trash can from his room with water and douses the fire. He goes back to bed. Later, the physicist wakes up and smells smoke. He opens his door and sees a fire in the hallway. He walks down the hall to a fire hose and after calculating the flame velocity, distance, water pressure, trajectory, etc., extinguishes the fire with the minimum amount of water and energy needed. Later, the mathematician wakes up and smells smoke. He goes to the hall, sees the fire and then the fire hose. He thinks for a moment and then exclaims, "Ah, a solution exists!" and then goes back to bed.

There were two men trying to decide what to do for a living. They went to see a counselor, and he decided that they had good problem-solving skills. He tried a test to narrow the area of specialty. He put each man in a room with a stove, a table, and a pot of water on the table.

He said, "Boil the water." Both men moved the pot from the table to the stove and turned on the burner to boil the water. Next, he put them into a room with a stove, a table, and a pot of water on the floor. Again, he said "Boil the water." The first man put the pot on the stove and turned on the burner. The counselor told him to be an engineer, because he could solve each problem individually. The second man moved the pot from the floor to the table, and then moved the pot from the table to the stove and turned on the burner. The counselor told him to be a mathematician, because he reduced the problem to a previously solved problem.

Twenty Things That Never Happen in Star Trek:

1. The *Enterprise* runs into a mysterious energy field of a type it has encountered several times before.
2. The *Enterprise* goes to visit a remote outpost of scientists, who are all perfectly fine.
3. Some of the crew uses the holodeck, and it works properly.
4. The crew of the *Enterprise* discovers a totally new life-form, which later turns out to be a rather well-known old life-form just wearing a funny hat.
5. The crew of the *Enterprise* is struck by a mysterious plague, for which the only cure can be found in the well-stocked *Enterprise* sick bay.
6. The captain has to make a difficult decision about a less advanced people, which is made a great deal easier by the Star Fleet Prime Directive.
7. The *Enterprise* successfully ferries an alien VIP from one place to another without a serious incident.
8. An enigmatic being composed of pure energy attempts to interface with the

Enterprise's computer, only to find out it has forgotten to bring the right leads.

9. A power surge on the bridge is rapidly and correctly diagnosed as a faulty capacitor by the highly trained and competent engineering staff.
10. The *Enterprise* is captured by a vastly superior alien intelligence, which they easily pacify by offering it some sweets.
11. The *Enterprise* is captured by a vastly superior alien intelligence which does not put it on trial.
12. The *Enterprise* visits an Earth-type planet called "Paradise" where everyone is happy all the time. However, everything is soon revealed to be exactly what it seems.
13. A major Starfleet emergency breaks out near the *Enterprise,* but fortunately, some other ships in the area are able to deal with it to everyone's satisfaction.
14. The *Enterprise* is involved in a bizarre time-warp experience which is in some way unconnected with the late twentieth century.
15. Kirk (or Riker) falls in love with a woman on a planet he visits, and isn't tragically separated from her at the end of the episode.

16. Counselor Troi states something other than the blindingly obvious.

17. The warp engines start playing up a bit, but seem to sort themselves out after a while without any intervention from boy genius Wesley Crusher.

18. Wesley Crusher gets beaten up by his classmates for being a smarmy goof, and consequently has a go at making some friends of his own age for a change.

19. Spock (or Data) is fired from his high-ranking position for not being able to understand the most basic nuances of about one in three sentences that any-one says to him.

20. Things that are new or in some way unexpected.

Mathematical Hot Air

Three men are in a hot air balloon. Soon, they find themselves lost in a canyon somewhere. One of the three men says, "I've got an idea. We can call for help in this canyon and the echo will carry our voices far."

So he leans over the basket and yells out, "Hellllooooooo! Where are we?" (They hear the echo several times.) About fifteen minutes later, they hear this echoing voice: "Hellllooooooo! You're lost!!"

One of the men says, "That must have been a mathematician."

Puzzled, one of the other men asks, "Why do you say that?"

The reply: "For three reasons. (1) He took a long time to answer, (2) he was absolutely correct, and (3) his answer was absolutely useless."

What is Pi?

Mathematician: Pi is the number expressing the relationship between the circumference of a circle and its diameter.

Physicist: Pi is 3.1415927 plus or minus 0.000000005.

Engineer: Pi is about 3.

Too Much Pi?

Q: What does a mathematician do when he's constipated?
A: He works it out with a pencil.

And Now, for a Really Bad Picture Joke

Q: What quantity is represented by this picture?

```
    /\       /\      /\
   /  \     /  \    /  \
  /    \   /    \  /    \
 /      \ /      \/      \
/______\ /______\/______\
   ||       ||      ||
   ||       ||      ||
```

A: 9, tree + tree + tree.

Q: A dust storm blows through, now how much do you have ?
A: 99, dirty tree + dirty tree + dirty tree.

Q: Some birds go flying by and leave their droppings, one per tree, what do you have now?
A: 100: dirty tree and a turd + dirty tree and a turd + dirty tree and a turd.

One for Escher Fans

Q: What's nonorientable and lives in the sea?
A: Mobius Dick.

A doctor, a lawyer, and a mathematician are sitting around talking about the benefits of having a wife versus a mistress.

The Perils of Professionalism

The lawyer says: "For sure a mistress is better. If you have a wife and want a divorce, it causes all sorts of legal problems."

The doctor says: "It's better to have a wife because the sense of security lowers your stress and is good for your health."

The mathematician says: "You're both wrong. It's best to have both so that when the wife thinks you're with the mistress and the mistress thinks you're with your wife—you can do some mathematics."

Proof Positive

Theorem: A cat has nine tails.

Proof: No cat has eight tails. A cat has one tail more than no cat. Therefore, a cat has nine tails.

Fore!

An assemblage of the most gifted minds in the world were all posed the following question: "What is 2 x 2?"

The engineer whips out his slide rule and shuffles it back and forth, and finally announces: "3.99."

The physicist consults his technical references, sets up the problem on his computer, and announces "It lies between 3.98 and 4.02."

The mathematician cogitates for a while, oblivious to the rest of the world, then announces: "I don't what the answer is, but I can tell you, an answer exists!"

A noted philosopher looks up and asks quizzically, "What do you mean by 2 x 2?"

The logician says "Please define 2 x 2 more precisely."

The computer hacker breaks into the NSA super-computer and gives the answer, "4."

The accountant closes all the doors and windows, looks around carefully, then asks, "What do you want the answer to be?"

How to Determine if Technology Has Taken Over Your Life

1. Your stationery is more cluttered than Warren Beatty's address book. The letterhead lists a fax number, E-mail addresses for two on-line services, and your Internet address, which spreads across the breadth of the letterhead and continues to the back. In essence, you have conceded the first page of any letter you write to your letterhead.

2. You can no longer sit through an entire movie without having at least one device on your body beep or buzz.

3. You need to fill out a form that must be typewritten, but you can't because there isn't one typewriter in the house—only computers with laser printers.

4. You think of the gadgets in your office as "friends," but you forget to send your father a birthday card.

5. You disdain people who use low baud rates.

6. When you go into a computer store, you eavesdrop on a salesperson talking

with customer—and you butt in to correct him and spend the next twenty minutes answering the customer's questions while the salesperson stands by silently, nodding his head.

7. You use the phrase "digital compression" in a conversation without noticing how strange your mouth feels when you say it.

8. You constantly find yourself in groups of people to whom you say the phrase "digital compression." Everyone understands what you mean, and you are not surprised or disappointed that you don't have to explain it.

9. You know Bill Gates' E-mail address, but you have to look up your own social security number.

10. You stop saying "phone number" and replace it with "voice number," since we all know the majority of phone lines in any house are plugged into contraptions that talk to other contraptions.

11. You sign Christmas cards by putting :) next to your signature.

12. Off the top of your head, you can think of nineteen keystroke symbols that are far more clever than :).

13. You back up your data every day.

14. You think jokes about being unable to program a VCR are stupid.

15. On vacation, you are reading a computer manual and turning the pages faster than everyone else who is reading John Grisham novels.

16. The thought that a CD could refer to finance or music rarely enters your mind.

17. You are able to argue persuasively that Ross Perot's phrase "electronic town hall" makes more sense than the term "information superhighway," but you don't because, after all, the man still uses hand-drawn pie charts.

18. You go to computer trade shows and map out your path of the exhibit hall in advance. But you cannot give someone directions to your house without looking up the street names.

19. You would rather get more dots per inch than miles per gallon.

20. You become upset when a person calls you on the phone to sell you something, but you think it's okay for a computer to call and demand that you start pushing buttons on your telephone to receive more information about the product it is selling.

21. You know without a doubt that disks come in 5¼ and 3½ inch sizes.

22. Al Gore strikes you as an "intriguing" fellow.

23. You own a set of itty-bitty screwdrivers and you actually know where they are.

24. While contemporaries swap stories about their recent hernia surgeries, you compare mouse-induced index-finger strain with a nine-year-old.

25. You are so knowledgeable about technology that you feel secure enough to say "I don't know" when someone asks you a technology question instead of feeling compelled to make something up.

26. You rotate your screen savers more frequently than your automobile tires.

27. You have a functioning home copier machine, but every toaster you own turns bread into charcoal.

28. You have ended friendships because of irreconcilably different opinions about which is better—the track ball or the track pad.

29. You E-mail this message to all your friends over the Net. You'd never get around to showing it to them in person. In fact, you have probably never met most of these people face-to-face.

30. You understand all the jokes in this message. If so, we suggest that, for your own good, you go lie under a tree and write a haiku. And don't use a laptop.